IMAGES OF ENGLAND

STAMFORD AND SURROUNDINGS

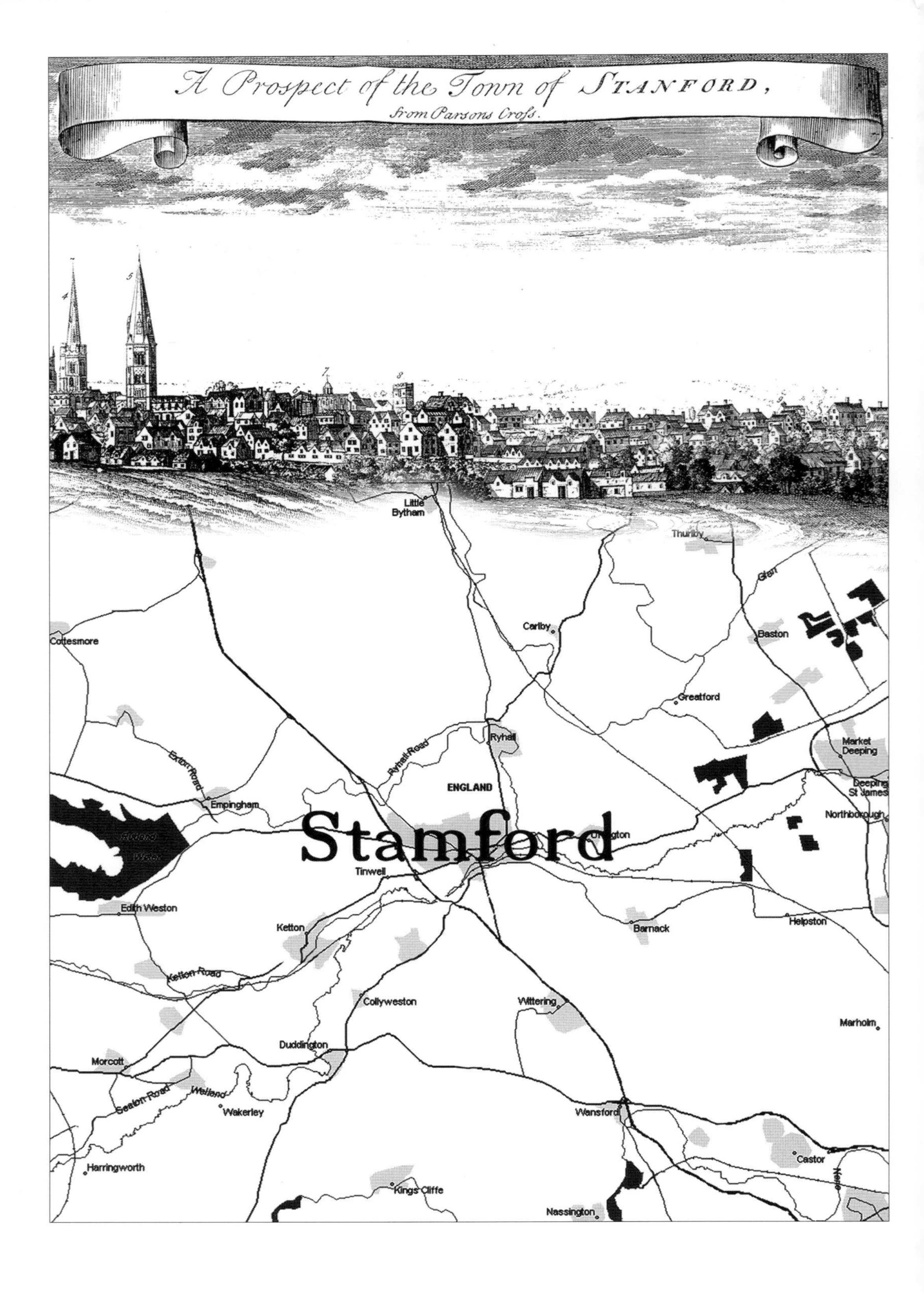

A Prospect of the Town of STANFORD,
from Parsons Cross.
Little Bytham
Thurlby
Glen
Carlby
Baston
Cottesmore
Greatford
Ryhall
Ryhall Road
Market Deeping
Exton Road
ENGLAND
Deeping St James
Empingham
Northborough
Stamford
Rutland Water
Tinwell
Edith Weston
Ketton
Barnack
Helpston
Ketton Road
Collyweston
Wittering
Marholm
Duddington
Morcott
Seaton Road
Welland
Wakerley
Wansford
Castor
Nene
Harringworth
Kings Cliffe
Nassington

IMAGES OF ENGLAND

STAMFORD AND SURROUNDINGS

BRIAN ANDREWS

TEMPUS

Frontispiece: This is part of a panorama from Francis Peck's *Antiquarian Annals of Stamford*, over a map showing Stamford and some of the villages included in this book.

First published 2006

Tempus Publishing Limited
The Mill, Brimscombe Port,
Stroud, Gloucestershire, GL5 2QG
www.tempus-publishing.com

British Library Cataloguing in Publication Data.
A catalogue record for this book is available from the British Library.

ISBN 0 7524 3845 X

Typesetting and origination by Tempus Publishing Limited.
Printed in Great Britain.

Contents

Acknowledgements

The majority of the photographs in this book are from the extensive collection at Stamford Museum. Many, however, have been provided by the kind generosity of private individuals, who were always more than willing to share their local knowledge and often amusing anecdotes with me.

I would like to express particular gratitude to Alan Tutt, Phil Massey and the staff at Stamford Museum and Library for their patience and support while compiling research for this book. I am also indebted to the following people: Mary-Anne Andrews, Gordon Barnes, Wendy Bell, Geoff Bladen, Jesse Brace, Canon John Bryan, Bob and Judith Chapman, Jill Clayton, David and Elizabeth Close, Collyweston Historical and Preservation Society, Hilda and Percy Halford, Peter Hankins and the people of Duddington village, John Hercock, Dr J. Hibble, Peter Hill, Steve Hutcheson, Desmond Knapp, Carol and David Lack, Una and Frank Lemon, Gilbert Markley, Sue and Richard Trow-Smith, Peter and Bobby Sanders, Claude Smith, Graham and Linda Worrell, Bob Wyles, and John and Margaret Young.

I am also grateful to Katherine Burton at Tempus Publishing for providing me with an outlet for my lifelong passion in historical research, and also for giving me a reason to make contact with so many wonderfully interesting people

Residents relax in the beautiful quadrangle garden of Browne's Hospital, *c.* 1890.

Introduction

Eighteen years ago, when I moved to a small village on the outskirts of Stamford in Lincolnshire, I was astounded that this jewel in middle England had remained unknown to me until then. This archetypal market town is surrounded by numerous rural communities, where much has remained the same for the past 300 years.

Characterised by its fine limestone buildings and uneven stone-slated roofs, the town is a monument to a heritage of craftsmanship and to those who had the foresight to preserve the work of the town's early artisans, keeping it relatively intact. The town lies at a point in south Lincolnshire which shares an approximate border with three other counties: Rutland, Cambridgeshire and Northamptonshire. I have chosen to include images from villages within these surrounding areas, in order to present a broad account of life in this part of the East Midlands during a period of great social change between 1860 and 1960.

My prime source for the images included in this book is the extensive collection held by Stamford Museum. Each village, however, has its own photographic archive maintained by amateur enthusiasts with a wealth of local knowledge. These have proven an invaluable source of reference to me during my hours of research. Many of the surrounding villages have a rich history in their own right. Great Casterton, to the north, was a Romano-British settlement before Stamford came into being. Collyweston, to the south, was home to Lady Margaret Beaufort, mother of Henry VII. All that remains on the site of her palace is an Elizabethan kitchen garden, fish ponds and a unique sundial of later origin. Further south is Fotheringhay, the birthplace of Richard III and the site where Mary Queen of Scots was executed. Next to the earth mound upon which Fotheringhay Castle once stood is a large piece of stone which was dedicated as a memorial to Richard III. Geddington, also in Northamptonshire, has one of the last remaining Eleanor crosses, erected to mark one of the twelve places where the wife of Henry II, Queen Eleanor's funeral procession stopped overnight on its way to Westminster Abbey.

The first records of Stamford date back to the ninth century when, together with Derby, Leicester, Lincoln and Nottingham, it became one the five controlling burghs of Danelaw. The town's name derives from a now-vanished stone ford which crossed the river Welland at a point close to the current town bridge where the flood plain is at its narrowest. It is commonly believed that Boudicca pursued the 9th Roman Legion across the river here, although there is no real evidence of this.

After the Romans had departured, Stamford became one of the first towns to adopt the skill of their Danish invaders by producing distinctive, wheel-turned, green-glazed pottery. Its relative durability has proven of great benefit to archaeologists investigating the subject.

Very little remains of the eleventh-century castle which once dominated Stamford. This old enclosure, from its tall elevation close to St Peter's church, held a strong defensive position overlooking the river. It was, nevertheless, besieged and captured by Henry of Anjou in 1135. The mound was finally levelled in 1935 to make way for a car park, which has now become the bus station.

There are early indications of affluence during the 200 years leading up to the twelfth century, when Stamford had a flourishing mint almost equal in output to that of London and York. However, the town's true prosperity came about in the thirteenth century due to its position on the Welland and close proximity to the agricultural resources of the nearby fenlands.

The local long-fleeced sheep produced wool of a very good quality. Stamford acted as a trading centre for this product, which was then exported to the continent to be woven into a high grade, durable fabric. Some of the wool remained to be woven into a renowned local textile known as Haberget. By the thirteenth century Stamford had become a byword for high quality material.

One of the most notable families who acquired their wealth through the wool trade were the Brownes. They were great beneficiaries, who lend their name to the imposing almshouse close to the centre of town. William Browne, who commissioned this building in 1475, also rebuilt the nearby All Saints' church during the same period. At the south-east end of the town, set within 1400 acres of surrounding parkland, is the magnificent Burghley House. This has been the home of the Cecil family since 1587, when it was built by William Cecil, lord high treasurer to Elizabeth I.

Stamford was sacked in 1461 by the Lancastrian army. This lead to a radical decrease in population that did not recover until the seventeenth century, when the town underwent some expansion within the confines of the medieval walls. This period of redevelopment also resulted in an increase in the number of skilled stonemasons whose expertise lead to a change in building styles in the area. Exposed timber-framing went out of fashion, to be replaced by stone re-fronting for those who could afford it. Other buildings were covered in lath and plaster. Despite this change in building style, the old layout of Stamford remained the same.

The eighteenth century witnessed the most radical change in the physical appearance of the town. Increased affluence and a plentiful supply of local stone lead to further refacing or reconstruction of many of the medieval buildings, in line with the fashions of the time. In most cases, thatched roofs disappeared after the town council of 1676 proposed that all houses should be covered in slates or tiles to prevent the risk of spreading fire. It is interesting to note that many of the houses still have a curfew window (from the old French *cuevrefeu*) built into the side of an inglenook fireplace, through which the shire reeve or sheriff could check that the fire had been extinguished for the night.

The declining demand for thatch lead to one of the most distinctive and characteristic features of the area; the Collyweston slate roof. Quarried mainly in Easton-on the-hill and Collyweston, from which it gets its name, this durable material has been in use since Roman times.

Stamford was the first town to be designated a conservation area in 1967.

Brian Andrews
Stamford, February 2006

one

Collyweston Slating

From quarrying to final dressing, the process of stone-slate roofing has always been a most specialist and labour-intensive skill. Even today, when only a limited number of people have the skills to undertake this work, most of the techniques and processes remain the same.

Collyweston slate begins life as a log of oolitic fissile limestone quarried from pits or 'foxholes' between thirty and sixty feet below ground. All of the work involved in getting these stone blocks was carried out by hand – an arduous, time consuming and potentially dangerous task.

Quarrying generally took place during the winter months when the freezing weather played its part in the slate-making process. The slate miner would lie on his side and chip away at the sand under the seam using a long-handled, pointed pick axe. Waste stone would be piled into columns to support the ceiling and the stone log, which would be tapped periodically to check when it was ready to fall. At this point, a series of clicks would be heard, warning the miners to retreat from the area before the seam gave way. If the stone did not fall, steel wedges would be driven into it before levering it away with a long iron bar known as a lion's tail.

In this image, *c.* 1932, William Knapp lies on his side in the cramped, claustrophobic conditions of a foxhole, using the traditional tool known as a foxing pick.

The fresh log was transported to the mouth of the pit on a flat wheelbarrow known as a 'shim', ready to be winched to the surface. In the picture above, *c.* 1935, William Knapp supports the freshly retrieved stone log while J. Stapleton helps to turn the hardwood windlass.

Once on the surface, the stone would be laid out on a bed of shale and kept damp by constant dowsing in water. The freezing frost would then open naturally occurring fissures in the rock, allowing the skilled mason to split it into sheets of approximately 7mm thickness. This frosting technique was discovered in the sixteenth century. Before this slates could be up to 20mm in thickness. In this image, *c.* 1930, Hugh Harrod demonstrates the traditional method of cliving slates by using a heavy cliving hammer to prise apart the naturally occurring stone stratifications.

After splitting, the slates were dressed into various sizes, the greatest skill being to produce the largest possible slate from the source stone. The slater would be skilful in the use of a batting or dressing hammer, to produce a rectangular slate with the characteristic rough edges which contribute to the pleasing appearance of a Collyweston slate roof. Holes were drilled using a primitive tool known as a bill and helve. This was usually a sharpened file inserted crudely though a wooden handle. This is a picture, *c.* 1930, of a gang of slaters posing with the tools of their trade. From left to right, back row: A. Osbourne, W. Smith, -?-, -?-, -?-. Front row, from left: A Walton, M. Harrod with a batting or dressing hammer, -?- with a bill and helve, R. Close (Long Dick), and A. Harrod with a cliving hammer.

The slaters worked on a patch protected from the elements by a thatch hurdle known as a 'house'. This picture shows two slaters behind the shelter which afforded them protection from the sun in summer and the freezing winds of winter. Arthur Woods, on the right of the picture, is using a bill and helve to make holes in the slates for pegging to the roofing lathes or 'witnesses'. The trade directories of this period make frequent references to 'traymakers'. These were in fact hurdle makers who constructed the 'houses' and other wattle structures for fencing and so on in the 1930s.

After dressing and drilling, the slates were laid out in a slater's thousand, which contained 840 slates. Each slate size had a unique name according to its size and position on the roof.

J.R. Harrod and J. Knapp with Knapp & Sons' horse-drawn slating wagon known in the trade as a 'trolley', *c.* 1910.

E. Knapp and R. Woods re-slating the roof of Easton-on-the-Hill School, *c.* 1930. The rack at either end of the plank could be adjusted to accommodate the angle of the roof. A Collyweston roof usually needed to have a pitch of forty-seven degrees in order to prevent wind damage and to maximise rain flow from its surface. Below are listed the slate sizes and names, starting from the apex of the roof: 6in: 'Even Mope'; 6½in: 'Large Mope'; 7in: 'Even Mumford'; 7½in: 'Large Mumford'; 8in: 'Even Job'; 8½in: 'Large Job'; 9in: 'Even Short-Un'; 9½in: 'Large Short-Un'; 10in: 'Even Long-Un'; 10½in: 'Large Long-Un'; 11in: 'Even Shortback'; 11½in: 'Large Shortback'; 12in: 'Even Middleback'; 12½in: 'Large Middleback'; 13in: 'Even Longback'; 13½in: 'Large Longback';14in: 'Batchelor'; 15in: 'Wibbett'; 16in: 'Twelve'; 17in: 'Fourteen'; 18in: 'Sixteen'; 19in: 'Eighteen'; 20in: 'In-Bow'; 21in: 'Out-Bow'; 22in: 'Short Ten'; 23in: 'Middle Ten'; 24in: 'Long Ten'.

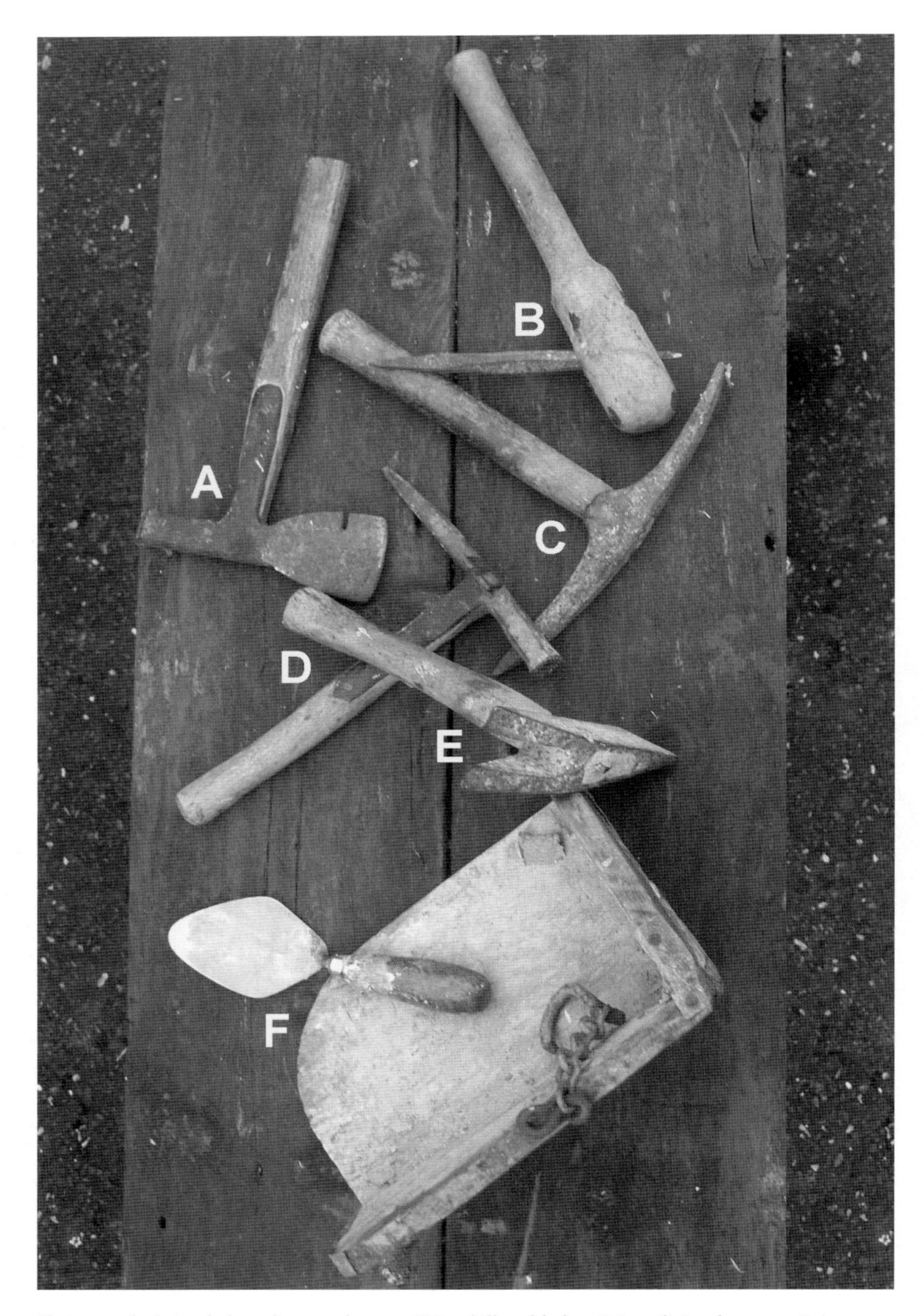

Slating tools: A is a lathe splitter and cutter, B is a bill and helve, C is a cliving hammer, D is a slater's pick, E is a dressing hammer, F is a trowel and hod with an attached chain for hanging from a roof ladder.

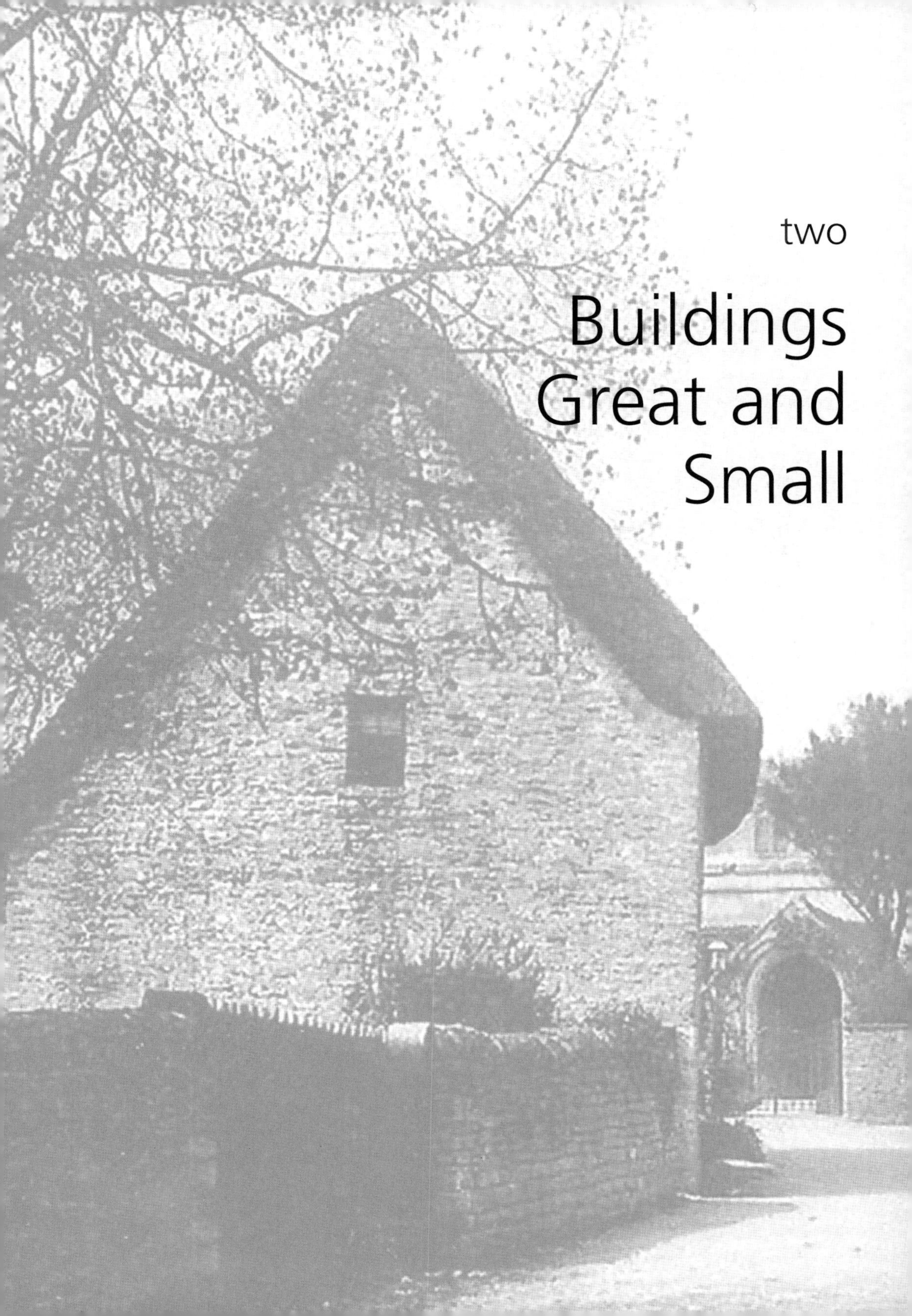

two

Buildings Great and Small

Cottage in Church Lane, Duddington, *c.* 1906. This rare example of thatched roofing in the area was demolished in 1932 to make way for the present village hall. Mrs King lived in the house on the right of the picture.

An etching of Stamford Castle, published by R.A. Ackerman, *c.* 1816.

Despite their ecclesiastical appearance these three Norman arches, since filled in, would have originally provided access to the buttery or bottle room of the castle, from which wine or other provisions would be dispensed. This was taken in around 1881.

This drawing is of Burghley House, *c.* 1850. Some of the fine gardens which were designed by Lancelot 'Capability' Brown, only a few years before this date, are clearly evident on the right of the picture.

Hilda and Percy Halford at No. 8 High Street, Collyweston, *c.* 1989. This sundial, which contains the cryptic message 'I ray for no man', became detached from the building on Christmas Eve, yet remarkably suffered no damage. It was restored to its position on the front of the house soon afterwards.

This is a recent photograph of a unique sundial which stands in the gardens of the now-demolished Collyweston Palace. Although later in origin than the original building, it is one of the few remaining architectural features on the site. Burghley Estates recently replaced the gnomon, and it now displays an accurate representation of the time of day in the concave feature at the head of the structure.

Collyweston Manor House, shortly after removal to its present location, where it was extended. The original house, which dates from 1696, was moved in its entirety from the High Street to the main road in around 1919. Major V.H. Bailey, who undertook this work, remained a resident in the house until the 1980s.

An aerial view, *c.* 1940, of Blatherwycke Hall in Northamptonshire. This splendid Georgian house was completed in 1724 for the vast sum of over £3,838. After use and abuse by the military in the Second World War it was eventually demolished in 1948. A few of the surrounding outbuildings are all that remain of this magnificent example of eighteenth-century architecture.

A late seventeenth-century drawing of Wothorpe Hall. This beautiful Elizabethan lodge, which is sited on land to the south of Stamford, once belonged to the Cecil family. It now lies in ruin after its abandonment during an outbreak of cholera and typhoid in the eighteenth century. 'Capability' Brown reused most of the salvaged materials for the building of a new stable block and additional architectural features at Burghley House.

Normanton Hall and church, *c.* 1906. Most of this area is now submerged under Rutland Reservoir, which was completed in 1977 engulfing 3,100 acres of the county of Rutland, including the village of Normanton, which disappeared beneath the water.

William Goddard-Jackson and family at the gates of their home in Duddington Manor, *c.* 1895.

Above left: This photograph, *c.* 1960, shows a south-facing, first-floor, stone-mullioned window from Stock's Hill House, Duddington. The stone above is all that remains of a sundial. There is also a date stone from around 1601. The word 'mullion' refers to the vertical member between the lights in a window opening. This can be made in shaped wood or, as in the example above, of carved stone.

Above right: This fifteenth-century door, pictured here *c.* 1950, was moved from its original position at Nos 46-47 High St (which were demolished in 1966), to its present location in the east wall of the seventeenth-century building at Nos 5-6 Maiden Lane.

This door and accompanying porch at 12 Barn Hill, pictured here *c*. 1950, date from around 1700. This is an example of a timber-framed house with a reconstructed stone frontage, in line with the fashion of the late seventeenth century. This main doorway has a curved pediment suspended on elaborately carved console brackets.

This classical Georgian-style door at 20 St Mary's Street, pictured here *c*. 1950, dates from the mid-eighteenth century. This property was enlarged and re-fronted together with others in the area in eighteenth and nineteenth centuries, reflecting Stamford's increasing wealth and expansion during this period.

Stamford Public Baths, *c.* 1950. This was built in 1823 to replace an earlier building from 1722. William Lowson, the first bath keeper, provided an invaluable service for those without the rare benefit of a private bathroom in their own home.

Rose Cottage, ? Street, Duddington, *c.* 1890s. This was the home of Mrs Hudson, who can be seen in the foreground. Further on is the Methodist Chapel, which has now been demolished.

A drawing of the medieval town bridge from Francis Peck's *Antiquarian Annals of Stanford*, *c.* 1715. The bridge incorporated five arches and a gateway, over which stood the town hall. The gate was demolished in 1778 by the Wansford Road Turnpike Trust.

Above: A photograph of the current town bridge, *c.* 1909. The old bridge was replaced in 1849 by a new one built to the designs of Edward Browning, a prominent Stamford architect. A new town hall was built further up St Mary's Hill.

Right: Brookes Court off Old Barn Passage, leading to Bath Row, *c.* 1865. William Studwell, cabinet maker, wood turner, French polisher and undertaker had his workshop here from 1850 until the 1870s.

Easton House decorated for the jubilee, *c.* 1897. Neville Day was born at Collyweston House in March 1842. He was manager of a number of estates including that of the Earl of Westmoreland, at Apethorpe. He commissioned the building of Easton House in 1870, where he lived until his death in 1925. He carried out a number of public works in Easton-on-the-Hill, including the installation of a water supply in 1888. The grounds of his house were given over to celebrations for Queen Victoria's Diamond Jubilee. The house is now used as a local office for the Institute of Purchase and Supply.

Tixover Group in street outside the newly built houses. From left to right: Michael Goddard-Jackson, Ken Gregory, Arthur Sauntson, Una Lemon and Betty Dawson (Aunt Bet).

three

Shops and Businesses

Red Lion Square, *c.* 1909. Red Lion Square was the commercial centre of Stamford as early as the twelfth century. The open stalls of the white meat market were eventually covered and became permanent shops in the eighteenth century. The Square derives its name from the former Red Lion Inn at No. 2, which was demolished in the early eighteenth century.

Rees Chemist, 6 Red Lion Square, *c.* 1875. One of their advertisements was, 'Scab! Scab! Scab! Rees castor oil sheep ointment.' Thomas George Rees, chemist and druggist, set up his shop in Red Lion Square in 1875. He continued until 1900 when the shop was bought by Freeman, Hardy & Willis' shoe shop, which traded continuously from this site until the 1990s.

Herding sheep into Sheepmarket, *c.* 1905. Many of the surrounding fields remained unenclosed until a relatively late date. Farming formed a central part of the economy of this small market town.

Star Tea Stores, 12 High Street, *c.* 1900, grocers and tea merchants under the management of Mr A. Taylor. Continued to trade until 1970. The Halifax Building Society now occupies the site.

Brown's butcher's shop, 60 High Street, *c.* 1910. Richard Henry Brown ran his butchery business here from 1900 to 1920 when the shop was taken over by John Grant, who was the last in a line of butchers stretching back 100 years. Woolworth's acquired the shop in 1936 with the intention of demolishing it along with the neighbouring property to make room for their latest store. The shop was eventually dismantled and re-erected in York Museum to become part of the 'bygones' collection, inaugurated by the well-known antiquarian D. Kirk. It now forms part of the exhibit known as Kirkgate and is a tribute to the man who had the vision and foresight to recognise the value of preserving such a monument for future generations. The *Stamford Mercury*, of 17 January 1936, expressed 'a pang of regret' at the loss of such an interesting piece of architecture and a valuable part of Stamford's heritage. Thankfully, Stamford's designation as a conservation area in 1967 called a halt to further commercial vandalism.

Jack Colson's butchers shop, Church Street, Easton-on-the-Hill, *c.* 1910. After serving an apprenticeship with Mr Tippings in Barnack, Jack Colson set up his own shop in Easton-on-the-Hill. Mr Colson is in the striped apron and Norman Wilds, the butcher's boy, is on the right.

Claypole & Coley, No. 1 Red Lion Square, *c.* 1879. Purveyors of musical instruments and later wirelesses. One of their advertisements was, 'Super-radio with super service. Free demonstration in your own home'. Pianos ranged in price from £18 18s to £36 15s and organs from £5 5s to £18 18s. Claypole & Coley continued to trade until the 1950s.

Cumberland's, family grocers, No. 4 St Martin's Street, *c.* 1930. Their slogan was, 'Cumberland's tea specially blended to suit the water of the district, 8d per ¼lb'. In 1900 John Colston Cumberland acquired No. 4 High Street, St Martin's. The Cumberland brothers set up a reputable family grocery business which lasted for over 100 years and was eventually extended into the neighbouring properties, Nos 5-6. They sent agents out to the surrounding villages to collect orders which were promptly despatched by horse and cart. Mr Cox, the agent for Duddington village, had a remarkable skill for pencilling down orders as fast as the customer could speak.

Mr E.H. Sneath and his shop assistant outside his Family Grocers and Italian Warehouse at No. 7, Scotgate.

S.J. Grimes of No. 14 St Mary's Street. This display was presented at the Chamber of Trade Exhibition, *c*. 1933. Sidney Grimes was the last in a long line of ironmongers to trade from this property. As was the practice of the time, within this Aladdin's cave of hardware he sold nails and screws by weight.

Left: W. Middleton, tailor and clothier, of No. 30 Broad Street, 'Begs most respectfully to thank the clergy, gentry and inhabitants of Stamford and vicinity for increasing patronage accorded to him since his removal into Broad Street, and hopes by strict and personal attention to all orders entrusted to him to receive continuance of the same.' This picture is from around 1880. William Middleton remained living and working here until 1900, when the shop was taken over by J.H. Woods, cabinet maker.

Below: R. Barton, confectioner, fancy bread and biscuit maker, St Mary's Hill, *c.* 1920. 'Muffins and crumpets daily' was their slogan and Richard Luke Barton set up his bakery business here in 1870. The shop continued to trade for over 100 years, eventually closing in the 1990s.

Above: Dolby Brothers, Nos 66-67 High Street, printers, bookbinders, stationers and booksellers, *c.* 1900. In the 1860s, William Dolby set up his business which remained here for over 100 years. The firm is most notable for producing an annual almanac and business directory from 1869 until the 1970s, which is a valuable source of reference to local historians and genealogists.

Right: Jenkinson's Printers and Stationers, High Street, *c.* 1895: 'Machine printing by atmospheric power'. In the 1870s George Jenkinson set up his printing and bookbinding business at 58 High Street and traded until 1900, during which time he produced a yearly trade directory similar to that produced by Dolby. Included among their numerous products was the 'Queen's album containing 12 lithographic views of Stamford and neighbourhood in neat case 1s.'

High Street delivery 1 July 1905. Taylor Downes, booksellers and stationers of Nos 51-53 High Street, were established on this site in 1900 where they remained for twenty-five years. Gleadall, who occupied No. 54 next door was a firm of coopers, cork factors and general wood carvers and turners. As well as this, they produced garden sieves 'from hair or wire' and monograms carved to any pattern.

Duckett's, *c.*1905. In 1900 Thomas Duckett, a grocer and coffee merchant, moved from No. 20 High Street and re-established his general provisions warehouse at No. 55. He advertised, among his many fine foodstuffs, 'fish at reasonable prices from Grimsby every morning'.

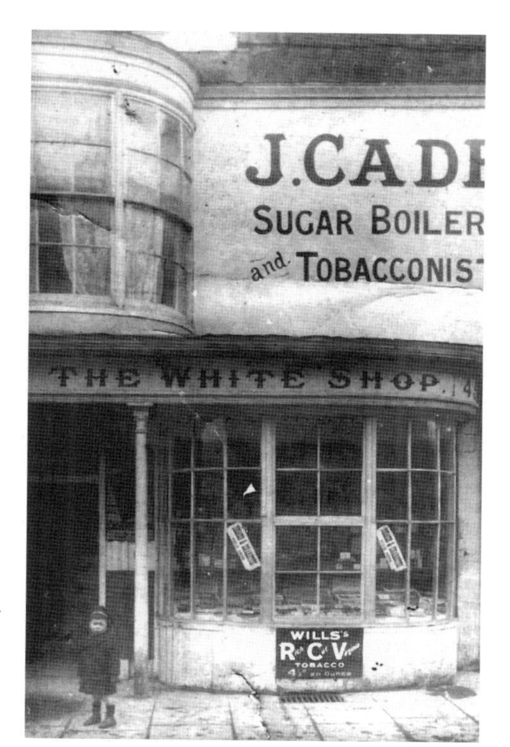

Cade's, confectioners of No. 45 High Street (next door to the entrance of Albert Hall), *c.* 1930. Charles Cade started his bakery and confectionery business in 1925 and later moved to No. 40 High Street to become Marshall's cake shop.

Tack Shop, No. 6 High Street, Collyweston, *c.* 1933. This was run by Frank Bonner, saddler and harness maker, from 1932-38.

Kate Perkins' general grocery store in the Steward's House, No. 28 High Street, Collyweston, *c.* 1923. From left to right, back row: Ginny Harrison holding baby, Colin Perkins, Elizabeth Close, -?-, -?-, Miss Heys, Jack Rogers, Arthur Close. Middle row: Jack Perkins, Kate Rogers, K. Perkins, Dolly Rodgers. Front row: Fred Jones, Mercy Perkins, Tom Jones. Kate Perkins died from blood poisoning in 1930 after pricking her finger with a sewing machine needle and then wearing a new pair of kid gloves which infected the wound. This was before the days of antibiotics which would undoubtedly have saved her life.

Opposite above: Ironmonger Street, *c.* 1906. Mr R. Islip is standing in the doorway of Knott's warehouse on the left of the picture. Pinney & Sons, next door, were jewellers, watchmakers, stationers and booksellers here until 1900 when they moved their business to No. 3 Red Lion Square.

Opposite below: W. & J. Brown, nurserymen, No. 56 High Street, *c.* 1905. William and James Brown moved here from No. 39 Broad Street in 1875. They sold un-packeted seeds, weighed out for the customer, from wall cabinets and drawers behind the counter. The business continued on this site until the 1970s.

PINNEY & SONS
Ironmonger St

SEED MERCHANTS
AND NURSERYMEN

Mr Fracey of Market Deeping, pictured here at the turn of the twentieth century, is skinning eels for sale outside Browne's Hospital in Broad Street.

This is a photograph of the last cattle market on Broad Street, *c.* 1896, before it moved across to the other side of the river, taking with it the clientele from local shops and inns.

Easton-on-the-Hill post office, *c.* 1910. This has recently been converted into a private residence, but the post box, which protrudes through the living room wall, remains in use.

Easton-on-the-Hill post office interior, *c.* 1910. R. Walter, J. Colson (butcher), Mrs Fahie and C. Fahie are in the background.

Duddington post office, between the wars. Mr and Mrs Brewster were the postmaster and mistress during this period. The local postman is said to have been an amputee who rode his bicycle and delivered letters with a hook replacing his missing limb.

Kingscliffe post office, on the corner of Forest Approach and West Street, with the Turner's Arms Inn opposite, *c.* 1905. Mr Albert Robinson Bailey was sub-postmaster here until 1941.

Above: Sarah Close outside the old post office at No. 5 High Street, Collyweston, *c.* 1901. Miss Close became the village postmistress after the retirement of Jane Scotney in 1899. She remained in the job until 1953.

Right: A Close baker, *c.* 1910. Bread was baked here on Monday, Wednesday, Friday and Saturday. On Sundays the ovens were reserved for outside baking, when villagers would bring their roasts, puddings and pies in to be baked in the huge oven that occupied the far end of the bake house. The cost was 1d for a milk pudding, ¾d for a pie and 2d for a cake or Sunday roast.

The Portico, pictured here *c.* 1900, was built in 1808 on the site of the old White Lion Inn as a butcher's shambles to house 53 covered stalls selling fish, white meat and dairy produce. It was built, from designs by William Legge, as a Tuscan portico, and was influenced by Covent Garden church in London. It was the site on which the hustings for the 1830 general election in Stamford took place. After a heated exchange, Charles Tennyson, uncle of the Poet Laureate, was challenged to a dual by his rival candidate; Colonel Thomas Chaplin. Shots were exchanged in a field near Wormwood Scrubs, but neither party suffered injury. By the end of the nineteenth century, when shambles had become dilapidated and unsuitable for its purpose, the council made the decision to fill in the arches and convert the building to become a library, fronting onto the High Street. The wing on either side of the portico housed the police station and the beadle's house. The northern end in Broad Street became the Stamford Technical School, which now houses Stamford Museum. The conversion cost £2,500, which was paid for by a grant from the Andrew Carnegie Trust.

four

Transport

Cecil Hemsell's ice cream van, Ketton, in the 1940s. Mr and Mrs Hemsell ran their sweetshop and ice cream factory from a small shed behind their house in Luffenham Road, Ketton. Mr Hemsell sold the confectionery around the villages from his mobile ice cream van.

Alf Hemfrey's grocery van. Alf and Flo Hemfrey ran their small grocery shop from the old schoolmaster's house next to the village hall in Collyweston. Alf's father, who shared his Christian name, set up the business in 1931 after losing his leg in a farming accident.

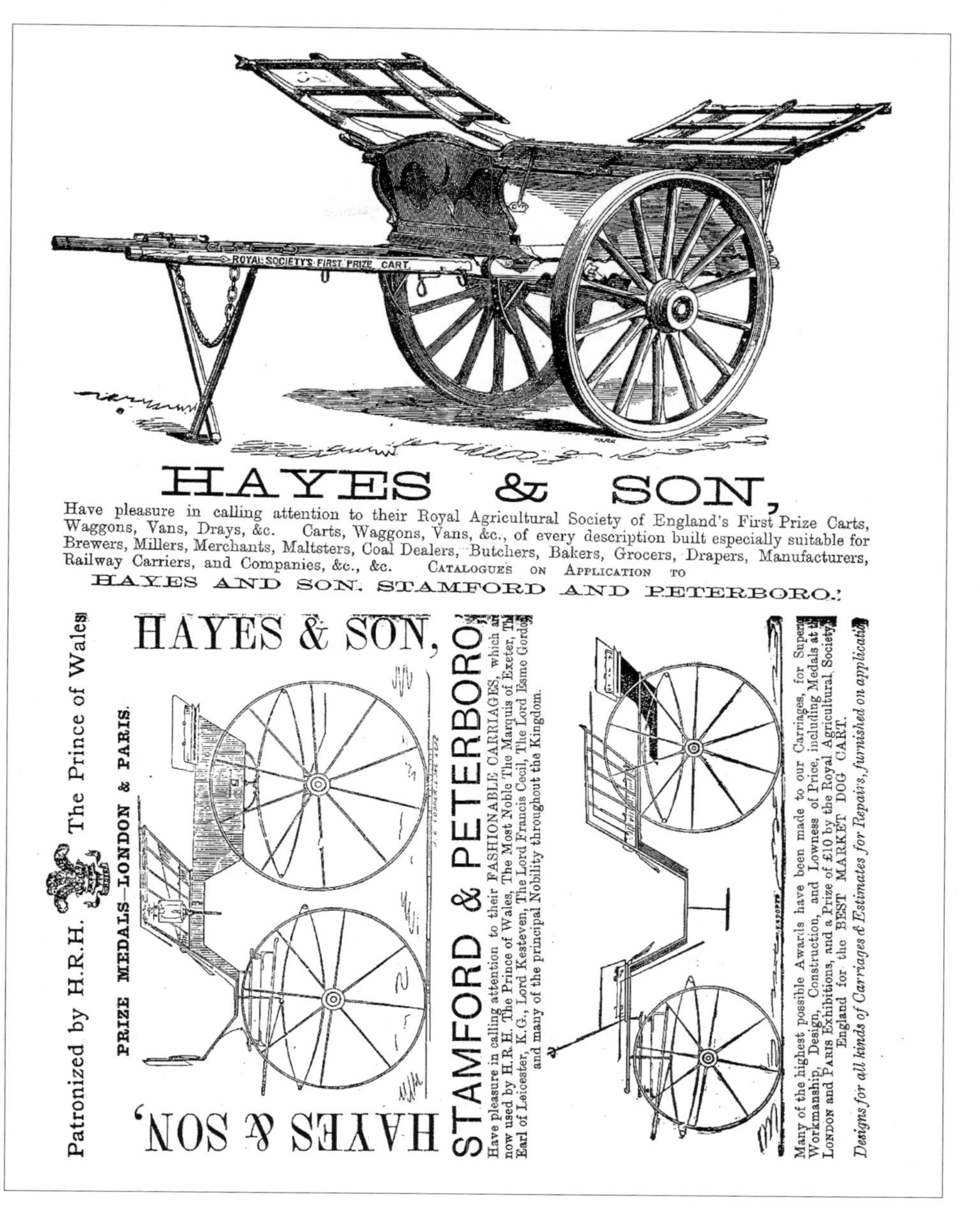

Hayes' wagons advertisement. In 1875, John Hayes & Son bought Nos 11-12 Scotgate from Mary Anne, daughter of William Spencer, and established a wagon-making business on the site. They built new showrooms and workshops where they continued to manufacture a range of horse-drawn vehicles for the next fifty years. They made Broughams (a light single-horse carriage); wagonettes; park, wire and other phantoms; Superior Whitechapel and other dog carts. These were all built to order or kept in stock. The products manufactured by this company ranged from heavy duty, functional coal wagons for both the GNER and the Midland Railway companies, to a highly decorative rhinoceros wagon for Wombwell's Menagerie. When the Crimean War broke out they received an order for a number of wagons from HM Board of Ordnance. It became a fire station in the 1920s when Hayes moved to Radcliffe Road.

Duddington Manor carriage, in the 1890s. It was the highest quality mode of transport in its day. This carriage was owned by local landowner William Goddard-Jackson, whose family lived in the manor until the 1990s. The Lord of Duddington Manor, Edward Philip Monckton, lived at Fineshade Abbey.

Close Bakery's delivery cart, outside the home and bakery in Collyweston. On the left is the baker's boy who lived above the shop in Collyweston, Elizabeth Close in the white dress stands by the railings while her husband Arthur holds the horse's reins, ready to begin the day's deliveries. The bread was originally delivered around the village on a handcart known as a 'shin'. This had a high back and sides and was large enough to transport three baker's baskets. Later, when Arthur Close acquired a large horse and trap, the bakery was able to sell its wares further afield to the surrounding villages. During winter he would go to the blacksmith to have special nails inserted through the horseshoes to prevent them slipping on ice.

Barrowden Pond and Village Green, *c.* 1910. The village pond at Barrowden once served a purely functional purpose. As well as a place for livestock to drink it was also used as a wagon wash. During hot weather, wagons would be driven into the water to cool down their metal rims or 'tyres', thus preventing them from detaching from the wheel due to expansion.

Above left: Romany caravans at Stamford Market, at the turn of the twentieth century. Kingscliffe woodworkers were among the crafts-people who relied upon travelling people to distribute their wares further afield. Kingscliffe was an 'open' village, with no resident lord of the manor. An altruistic local theologian, William Law, proved a great attraction to these itinerant folk.

Above right: William Miles of St John's Street, in a wicker bath chair at the Oakham Show, *c.* 1906.

Above: A GNER wagon at Stamford Easton Station, in the early twentieth century. The station was believed to be built by Haynes at the turn of the twentieth century.

Below: Sam Smith making local deliveries in the butcher's van, *c.* 1928.

Right: Jack Pick road tests his first car on Priory Road, *c.* 1900. John Henry (Jack) Pick set up his car production plant in Stamford on 19 March 1900. His first car in this picture was really just a dog cart with a four-and-a-half horsepower engine attached.

Below: Advertisement for Pick Cars, in front of the 'Bottle' Lodges of Burghley House, *c.* 1915. After a rift between Jack Pick and his company board, he set up an alternative business under the name New Pick.

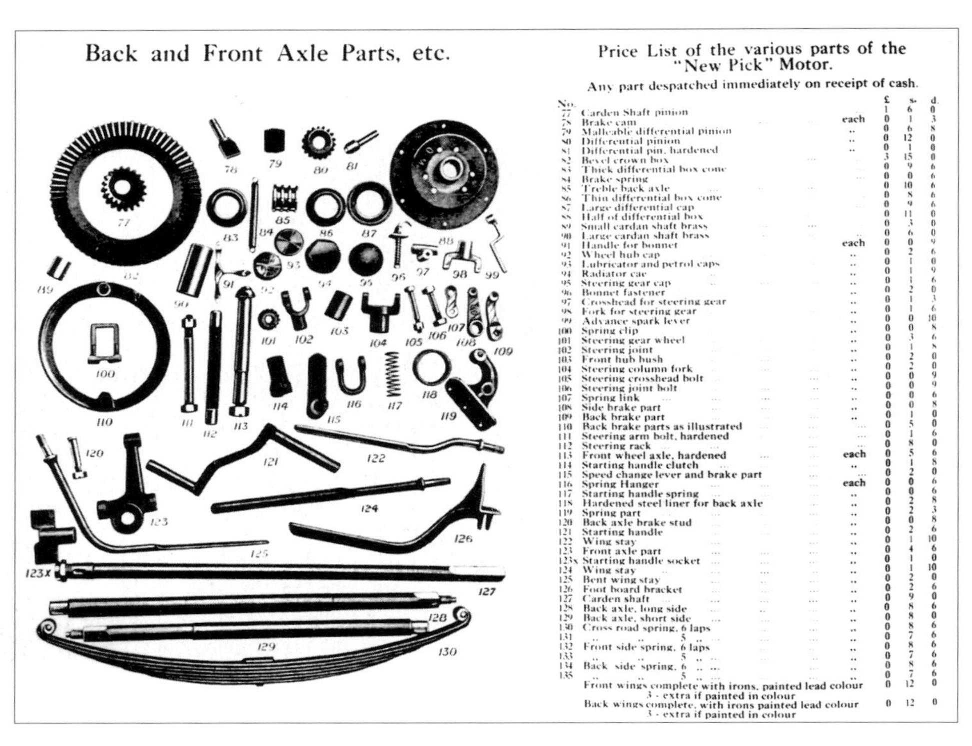

Back and Front Axle Parts, etc.

Price List of the various parts of the "New Pick" Motor.

Any part despatched immediately on receipt of cash.

No.			£	s.	d.
77	Carden Shaft pinion		1	6	0
78	Brake cam	each	0	1	3
79	Malleable differential pinion	..	0	6	8
80	Differential pinion	..	0	12	0
81	Differential pin, hardened	..	0	1	0
82	Bevel crown box		3	15	0
83	Thick differential box cone		0	9	6
84	Brake spring		0	0	6
85	Treble back axle		0	10	6
86	Thin differential box cone		0	8	6
87	Large differential cap		0	9	6
88	Half of differential box		0	11	0
89	Small cardan shaft brass		0	3	0
90	Large cardan shaft brass		0	6	0
91	Handle for bonnet	each	0	0	9
92	Wheel hub cap	..	0	2	6
93	Lubricator and petrol caps	..	0	1	0
94	Radiator cac	..	0	1	9
95	Steering gear cap	..	0	1	6
96	Bonnet fastener	..	0	2	0
97	Crosshead for steering gear	..	0	1	3
98	Fork for steering gear	..	0	1	6
99	Advance spark lever	..	0	0	10
100	Spring clip	..	0	0	8
101	Steering gear wheel	..	0	3	6
102	Steering joint	..	0	1	8
103	Front hub bush	..	0	2	0
104	Steering column fork	..	0	2	0
105	Steering crosshead bolt	..	0	0	9
106	Steering joint bolt	..	0	0	9
107	Spring link	..	0	0	6
108	Side brake part	..	0	0	8
109	Back brake part	..	0	1	0
110	Back brake parts as illustrated		0	5	0
111	Steering arm bolt, hardened		0	1	6
112	Steering rack		0	8	0
113	Front wheel axle, hardened	each	0	5	6
114	Starting handle clutch	..	0	1	8
115	Speed change lever and brake part		0	2	0
116	Spring Hanger	each	0	0	6
117	Starting handle spring	..	0	0	6
118	Hardened steel liner for back axle	..	0	2	8
119	Spring part	..	0	2	3
120	Back axle brake stud	..	0	0	8
121	Starting handle	..	0	2	6
122	Wing stay	..	0	1	10
123	Front axle part	..	0	4	6
123x	Starting handle socket	..	0	1	0
124	Wing stay	..	0	1	10
125	Bent wing stay	..	0	2	0
126	Foot board bracket	..	0	2	6
127	Carden shaft	..	0	9	0
128	Back axle, long side	..	0	8	6
129	Back axle, short side	..	0	8	0
130	Cross road spring, 6 laps	..	0	8	6
131	.. .. 5 ..	..	0	7	6
132	Front side spring, 6 laps	..	0	8	6
133	.. .. 5 ..	..	0	7	6
134	Back side spring, 6 ..	..	0	8	6
135	.. .. 5 ..	..	0	7	6
	Front wings complete with irons, painted lead colour 3 - extra if painted in colour		0	12	0
	Back wings complete, with irons painted lead colour 3 - extra if painted in colour		0	12	0

Pick's price list from the 1920s. The entire list adds up to £18 10s 11d at a time when the average minimum wage was £2 6s 10d for a forty-seven hour week.

Pick's Motor Works, No. 11 High Street, St Martin's, *c.* 1908. The garage carried out light repairs to motor vehicles and sold spare parts and accessories. It remained in these premises – across the road from the George Hotel – between the years 1905 and 1920.

St Martin's Garage, *c.* 1926, which was purchased by Charles Miles in 1925 after Pick's went into liquidation in the same year. This site is currently occupied by St Martin's Antique Centre.

Barnack's petrol forecourt and blacksmith's shop, in the 1930s. William Frederick Colson is outside the village blacksmith and wheelwright's shop in Barnack. As well as working as a farrier, Mr Colson maintained horse-drawn vehicles. However, with the coming of the motor car he set up a subsidiary to his business by dispensing fuel from the ancient pump in this picture.

Steamroller carrying out road maintenance on Station Road, Barnack, in the early twentieth century. The three girls to the far left are Vera, Rene and Freda Colson, daughters of the village blacksmith. The fourth child cannot be recognised.

Oates & Masson delivery vehicle, North Street, *c.* 1910. Oates & Musson were originally based in Broad Street from where they ran a complete house-furnishing and removals company. In 1880 they opened a vast department store and factory at No. 23 High Street. While their main business lay in antique restoration and furniture removal, as is evident from this novel form of transport, they expanded their business to become silk mercers, tailors, hatters, drapers and funeral furnishers. Later, the store was extended into Nos 23-24.

Stamford Ladies' Cycling Club, at the turn of the twentieth century. After the launch of the Starley and Sutton Safety Cycle in 1885, the sport became a popular pastime throughout the United Kingdom. During this period cycling clubs would organise regular outings into the surrounding countryside. The newly designed bicycle also allowed women to partake of the activity while preserving their modesty in ankle length skirts.

Harold Close outside the bicycle shop in Collyweston, in the 1940s. Harold's sons David and Don were charged with the task of delivering new bicycles up the very steep hill from Ketton Station. This would be achieved by riding one and pushing another alongside. Hercules cycles cost £3 19s 6d, with an additional 15s for a three-speed gear. With the growing popularity of this new craze, in the 1940s the shop converted to a wireless outlet. Accumulators (wireless batteries) could be recharged here for 9d.

Hugh Harrod on a Velocet motorcycle outside the newly built home of Bill and Monica Hercock in Slate Drift, Collyweston, February 27 1938.

Entrance to Barnack Station goods yard. The artist Wilfred Wood lived in the long house on the right of this picture.

Barnack bus, in around the 1930s or '40s. Patches' ran a local bus service from Stamford out to the surrounding villages. They also had a long-distance 'cream bus' service on which local children could take trips to the seaside. They were later replaced by Barton's Buses.

Newly constructed war memorial bus shelter at Wothorpe on the A43, *c.* 1921. This still exists on the A43 road into Stamford, opposite Second Drove.

Sergeant Stiff demonstrates kerb drill to the girls of All Saint's School, Scotgate, in the 1940s.

Lowe and Cobbold Brewery dray crashes into the front of Randall's shop at No. 6 St. John's Street after negotiating a treacherous bend, *c.* 1918.

Handley Page 50hp Heyford Bomber at Wittering RAF base family day, in the 1950s. The Heyford was the last of the RAF's biplane heavy bombers. It first flew in June 1930. Amazingly, for such a heavy aircraft, they were relatively easy to fly and could even be looped, a feat that was carried out at the 1935 Hendon Air Pageant.

May 25 1910, 'The ill fated carriers van'. This delivery wagon overturned on its way to Grantham in Lincolnshire after the horse bolted. Three people were killed and others were seriously injured.

Little Bytham train crash. On the night of 17 January 1936, the 5.30 p.m. express train from Leeds to London came to a disastrous end on a bridge outside Little Bytham. Its rear carriage left the rails, causing the brake van and several third-class compartments to fall onto the road below. Failure of the vacuum brake caused the engine to drag the damaged front carriage for half a mile down the track before grinding to a halt. There were two fatalities: Mrs Bligh from Pudsey in Yorkshire and Mr Michael Walter from London. Six others were seriously injured.

Above: Airship believed to be the R101 over St Andrew's church, Collyweston, in around 1929-30. The R101 was built at Cardington in Bedfordshire in 1929. At 777 feet in length it was the largest airship in the world.

Right: Memorial card issued after the R101 airship disaster on 4 October 1930. The airship left Cardington for Karachi in India. On board were forty-two crew, six officials and six passengers. After encountering difficulties due to high winds, the ship went into a steep dive, crashing into a hillside to the south-west of Beauvais in France. It quickly became engulfed in flames. Forty-six of those on board died immediately following the crash. Two others, crew members, died later of their injuries. There were only six survivors. This brought an effective end to British attempts at lighter-than-air aircraft.

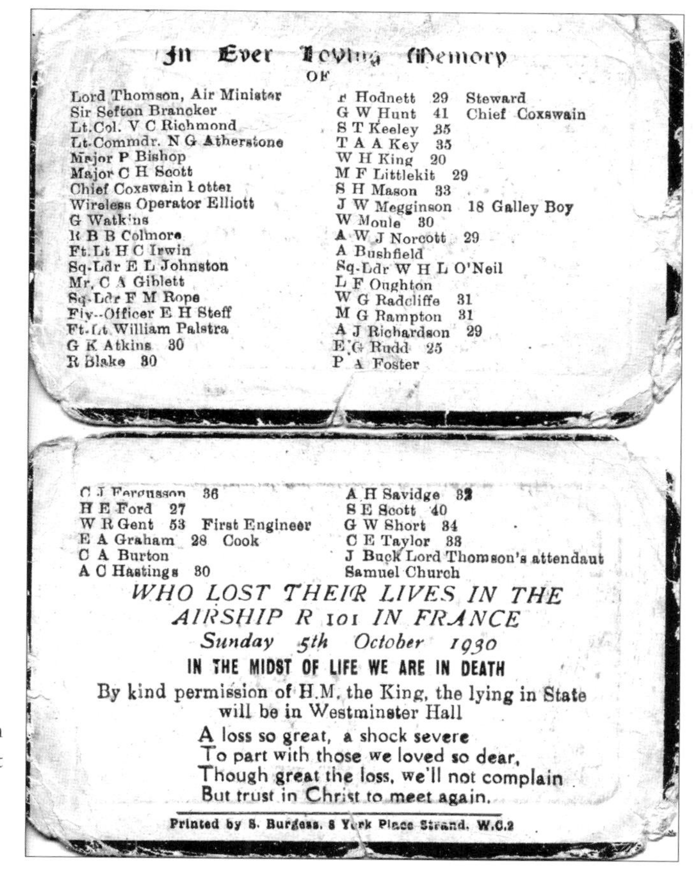

In Ever Loving Memory
OF

Lord Thomson, Air Minister
Sir Sefton Brancker
Lt.Col. V C Richmond
Lt-Commdr. N G Atherstone
Major P Bishop
Major C H Scott
Chief Coxswain Potter
Wireless Operator Elliott
G Watkins
R B B Colmore
Ft.Lt H C Irwin
Sq-Ldr E L Johnston
Mr. C A Giblett
Sq-Ldr F M Rope
Fly--Officer E H Steff
Ft-Lt William Palstra
G K Atkins 30
R Blake 30

F Hodnett 29 Steward
G W Hunt 41 Chief Coxswain
S T Keeley 35
T A A Key 35
W H King 20
M F Littlekit 29
S H Mason 33
J W Megginson 18 Galley Boy
W Moule 30
A W J Norcott 29
A Bushfield
Sq-Ldr W H L O'Neil
L F Oughton
W G Radcliffe 31
M G Rampton 31
A J Richardson 29
E G Rudd 25
P A Foster

C J Fergusson 36
H E Ford 27
W R Gent 53 First Engineer
E A Graham 28 Cook
C A Burton
A C Hastings 30

A H Savidge 32
S E Scott 40
G W Short 34
C E Taylor 33
J Buck Lord Thomson's attendant
Samuel Church

WHO LOST THEIR LIVES IN THE AIRSHIP R 101 IN FRANCE
Sunday 5th October 1930

IN THE MIDST OF LIFE WE ARE IN DEATH

By kind permission of H.M. the King, the lying in State will be in Westminster Hall

A loss so great, a shock severe
To part with those we loved so dear,
Though great the loss, we'll not complain
But trust in Christ to meet again.

Printed by S. Burgess, 8 York Place Strand, W.C.2

November 5 1937. This aircraft crash-landed in a field in Slate Drift, Collyweston, after the pilot, flight sergeant T.W. Newbold, and acting pilot, officer Farns, bailed out. The crew from RAF Wittering were practicing night flying around the airfield.

Bartfield C. Huck's monoplane, September 12 1912. Mr Huck, who was originally a test pilot for the Bradford Aircraft Company, operated from Burghley Park where he demonstrated flying and offered joyrides in his seventy-horsepower, two-seater Bleriot monoplane. This was the type of plane that Bleriot used to cross the channel three years before in 1909. During the First World War, the British and French used two-seater Bleriots for reconnaissance behind German lines. By 1915 however, they were outclassed by more advanced planes and were only used for ground training. Their wings were clipped to prevent them from taking off. Huck achieved fame in 1912 by being the first Englishman to demonstrate the loop-the-loop manoeuvre. He later went on to break a record by achieving thirty-three consecutive loops in one flight over Filey in Yorkshire.

five

Farming and Industry

Above: Jack Pick's first motor workshop in Blackfriar's street, *c.* 1905.

Below: Kitson's lighting workshop in Wharf Road, around the 1920s. Kitson's produced oil lamps until the Second World War, when they converted the factory into a militia works for the war effort.

Blackstone's original premises at Nos 41-42 Broad Street, *c.* 1900. Blackstone Engineering Co. was established by Henry Smith in 1837. The company was originally based in this late sixteenth-century jettied building in Broad Street. In 1913 they demolished this together with the neighbouring building and built a new three-storey showroom on the site, in which to display their agricultural equipment.

Lowe & Sons Brewers Ltd, St Michael's Brewery, Broad Street, around the 1890s. Established in 1819, it later became Lowe and Cobbold. The brewery occupied the site behind Browne's Hospital which later became Welland Motor Factory. An advertisement for the brewery read: 'Bottled AK Ale, Brown Ale and Oatmeal Stout 4s per dozen imperial pints.' In 1935 it was acquired by Holes of Newark.

Frank Hubbard shoeing a horse, *c.* 1978. Frank Hubbard became an apprentice blacksmith and farrier with his uncle Frank Tyler at the age of fourteen in 1921. His uncle was the blacksmith for both Collyweston and Easton-on-the-Hill. After completing his apprenticeship he worked for Burghley Estates for eighteen years before moving to Collyweston to take over his uncle's business. It was at this time that he moved the business away from its original site to a new workshop further down the road towards Duddington, where his daughter Judith still lives. As a village blacksmith he was able to supply the needs of a number of local industries, from wagon wheels to weathercocks. Also, crucially, he would produce some of the tools used by Collyweston slaters as well as the nails for fixing slates to roofs. As a farrier in those early days, he would be required to make horseshoes as well as fit them. He continued to work in this demanding, and at times dangerous, industry until his retirement at the age of seventy-five in 1982.

The original forge with Frank Tyler's car parked outside on the Stamford Road, *c*. 1940. Mrs Tyler ran a grocery shop from the house next door until the mid-1950s.

George Lemon and Bill Cunnington riding a horse-drawn hoe, Tixover, June 21 1938.

Horse-drawn reaper, Tixover, in the 1930s. The reaper was invented by Cyrus McCormac in 1834 and 100 years later the original design had barely changed, as can be seen in this photograph. The rotating blades cut the standing grain and deposited it onto a platform, from which it was raked by men walking alongside.

George Lemon, Stan Winkles (Winkie), -?- and Horace Pete bagging straw, Tixover, *c.* 1936.

Opposite above: George Close's hay wagon delivering to the baker's shop in Collyweston in the 1920s. Charlie Close is seated on the horse.

Kingscliffe woodturner, in the 1930s. William Bailey is working at his treadle lathe in his workshop behind the Turner's Arms in West Street. He was the last woodturner working in Kingscliffe.

STEAM TURNERY WORKS,

KING'S CLIFFE, Northamptonshire, ... 189

Mr. ....

Dr. to WILLIAM BOLLANS,

WOOD + TURNER + AND + CARVER.

Articles Manufactured and Sold by WILLIAM BOLLANS

per doz.

BUTTER PRINTS.
Common size, 1 oz.
Two ounce........
Quarter lb.........
Half lb. ....
One lb. ....

DITTO IN CASES.
Common size......
Two ounce........
Quarter lb.........
Half lb. ....
One lb. ....

BUTTER MOULDS.
Small size ....
Middle ....
Large ....

WOOD SPOONS.
Small ....
Nine-inch ....
Eleven and a half-inch Pudding
Twelve-inch Pickle
Fourteen-inch ....
Sixteen-inch ......
Eighteen-inch ....

per doz.

Twenty-inch ....
Twenty two inch

SCREW TAPS.
Small..............
Small Middle ....
Middle ....
Large ....
Extra ....

POWDER BOXES.
Three-in screw lids
Three and a half-in

SPICE BOXES.
Small 3-lift ......
Middle 4-lift ....
Common large 4-lift
Extra large 5-lift
Ditto 6-lift ......
Butter Runners ..

MISCELLANEOUS.
Scotch Hands ....
Potato Mashers ..
Lemon Squeezers
Yokes ....
Toys, sorted......
Varnished Pepper Boxes ....

per doz.

Varnished Salts....
Varnished Egg Cups
Quarter lb. Twine Boxes ....
Half lb. ....
One lb. ....
Lettered Bread Plates ....
Carved Plates ....
Plain Bread ditto..
Butter Boards and Knives ....
Wine Funnels ....
Vinegar Funnels ..
Punch Ladles ....
Salad Spoons and Forks ....
Turned Clothes Pegs
Spile Pegs........
Nutcracks ....
Nutmeasures ......
Watchmen's Rattles small ....
Ditto, middle ....
Ditto, large ......
Spell Cups........
Flour Dredgers....
Thirteen-in. Butter Knives ....
Nine-in. ditto ....
Eleven-in ditto....
Cash Bowls ....
Paste Boards......

per doz.

Small Cork Tap ..
Middle ditto......
White Egg Cups..
Four-in Toilet Dishes ....
Four and a half-inch Toilet Dishes ..
Shaving Boxes ..
Soap Dishes......
Three-inch Tooth Powder Boxes..
Carved Biscuit Rollers ....
Paste Rolling Pins
Small Crimping Boards & Rollers
Middle ditto......
Large ditto ......
Oval Butter Prints
Half-lb. ditto ....
One lb. ditto ....
Tun Dish Spouts..
Small Plain Taps
Middle ditto......
Large ditto ......
Half-pint Butter Churns ....
One pint ditto....
One quart ditto ..
Two-quart ditto ..
Money Boxes ....
Thimble Cases....
Skimming Dishes

Printed at the "Post" Printing Works. Stamford.

Featured is a product list and billhead, from the late nineteenth century, of William Bollins of Kingscliffe steam turnery. Originally, all woodturning was carried out on a 'pole lathe' which utilised the resilience of a long wooden pole embedded in the ground as its power source. Later, treadle lathes came into use and remained in some workshops until the 1930s. By this time, however, most turners were using steam to operate their lathes. With this method, local craftsman Levi Dixon (known as 'Old Crump') claimed that he was able to make 416 egg cups in eight hours. These were sold for 4s a gross. Mr Dixon died in 1907 aged seventy-five years. He was the last in a long line of woodturners in the Dixon family.

Opposite: Some examples of Kingscliffe turned woodwork, photographed by Ralph Hentall. The advent of aluminium in 1870 brought a rapid decline in the demand for ordinary domestic woodwork. By the early twentieth century, there were only six turners left in Kingscliffe.

Sugar beet labourers, Tixover, *c.* 1937. Harvesting sugar beet was a seasonal but fairly lucrative job. Although the roots could be lifted by a plough-like device which could be pulled by a horse team, the rest of the preparation was by hand. One labourer grabbed the beets by their leaves, knocked them together to shake free loose soil, and then laid them in a row, root to one side, greens to the other. A second worker equipped with a beet hook followed behind, and would lift the beet and swiftly chop the crown and leaves from the root with a single action. Working this way he would leave a row of beet that could then be forked into the back of a cart. From left to right: Mike Pete, -?-, Edgar Pete, Harry Pete, Jack Riley from Barrowden.

Barrowden Mill and Tannery, *c.* 1918. The first reference to a mill on this site is in 1259 when it was leased to Richard Gubiun at a rent of 40s per annum. This amount remained constant until it was sold to William and Margaret Dunmore in the late sixteenth century. A life insurance policy of 1778, when the mill was in the possession of Thomas Smith, placed the enormous value of £430, including stock and utensils, on the mill. The mill continued to work until the mid-1920s and remained standing in a ruinous state for many years after this. The tannery, which can be seen in the background, processed animal hides for rugs, glue and parchment for drums. The skins were washed and scraped to remove hair, after which they were whitened with pumice or chalk before being beaten into sheets. The tannery closed in 1885.

Ironstone workers, Easton-on-the-Hill, in the 1890s. Ironstone quarries were worked extensively in the Welland Valley below Easton-on-the-Hill during the last three decades of the nineteenth century. There was a special dock and siding built by the nearby railway to transport the ore to Frodisham in Lincolnshire. There was also a very steep, narrow gauge line through the nearby wood, some remains of which can still be seen. One man could operate this by standing on the rear car and using the brake and a lever for depositing the ironstone into a railway truck. On one occasion the brakes failed and fortunately the driver jumped free as the cars careered down the hill, smashing the telegraph lines and depositing their load on the tracks below. A disaster was averted as no train was due at the time. The private firm of Eldred's closed soon after to be taken over by the Marquis of Exeter from Burghley House. With a more efficient, mechanised approach, the industry was soon re-opened and continued to operate for several years after this.

six

Work and Play

Wood-carving class outside the old school room, Bridge Street, *c.* 1895. John J. Bailey, a highly skilled wood-carver and tutor of this class, is second from the left. Reverend Du Pre, the Rector of Kingscliffe at the time, stands on the left. The classes were organised at his instigation, as he was anxious to ensure that the skill of wood-carving was not lost in the village.

St Michael's School manual instruction class, *c.* 1913. St Michael's School, which was established in 1860 as a girls' school, continued until the early 1900s when it changed use to become a school for boys and later the Bluecoat School. Albert Francis is in the front row, as is 'Ginger' Barron and Alwyn Chatterton (wearing spectacles), son of the cobbler of Chapel Lane. The teacher is Mr Ellis. George Swanson is standing behind him.

This picture date from around 1900. The Stamford Scientific Institute was built on the site of the old Castle Inn, which was demolished in 1842. The curator at this time was Christopher Barnes Clarke who continued in this post until the 1870s. The architect was Bryan Browning who incorporated a number of classical features into its design, including the most unusual shaped front portal, which would appear to have been influenced by the tombs of Egypt. In this picture you can clearly see the octagonal observatory on its roof that contained a *camera obscura*. This was removed in 1910. Later, in the 1920s, the name changed to the Stamford Borough Club and it remained so until the 1950s when it became the YMCA. In more recent years it has been taken over by the Castle Hill Language School. The Russian 24-pounder cannon in the foreground was a trophy from the Crimean War and was melted down in 1940 for the war effort.

Language school billiard room, *c.* 1900. The Institute included a number of functions for both leisure and learning. Among these were a large concert and leisure hall, a games room, gallery, museum and library.

Gardening lessons at Easton-on-the-Hill School allotment, *c.* 1916. Second from the left is Clem Stuckey in a pullover. By the back wall in a white shirt is Bob Hubbard. Frank Hubbard, who later became the village blacksmith, is in the foreground with a garden fork.

Collyweston School Group, around the turn of the twentieth century. Lessons were fairly basic at that time, comprising mainly of the learning of the three 'R's: reading, writing and arithmetic. Classes 1 and 2 would be provided with a sand tray and later a pencil and slate on which to practice these skills. Classes 3 and 4 got a chalk and blackboard. At the top of the school, Classes 5 and 6 would finally be given proper writing implements – first a pencil, then a pen. Every day began with assembly, where silence was the order of the day. Punishment in the form of the cane or ruler would be swift and severe for anybody disobeying this rule.

Duddington School photograph, *c.* 1943. From left to right, back row: Pearl Pick (teacher), Ada Manton, Ron Prentiss, Margaret Chapman, Evelyn Bridges, Alan Massingham, Henry Manton, Garth Smith, Una Barfield, and Sally Abbot (headmistress). Second row: Barbara Ellis, Patsy Sanders, Jean Ellis, Barbara Rastall, Cissy Grey, Barbara Joins, Eileen Harrod, Edna Barfield, Thelma Smith. Third row: Honor Manton, Eric Wilkinson, Ron Sanders, Michael Ellis, Fred Compton, Freddy Hornsby, Vivian Hibbins, Henry Manton, Rosemary Wilkinson. Front row: Freddy Compton, Ray Smith, Barbara Pete, Hazel Ellis, Peter Sanders, Gordon Grey, Colin Grey.

Above: Kingscliffe May Day tableau, outside Kingscliffe Endowed School, *c.* 1916. Among the group are Mary Bailey and Marjorie Sharpe. Celebrations started at the school, where the girls had made posies of paper flowers to carry round the village on the morning of May Day, collecting pennies from the houses where they called. The maypole dancing also moved around, stopping at several places along the village streets which 100 years ago had no motor vehicles to worry the dancers.

Easton-on-the-Hill, May Day, *c.* 1924. The first of May was always an eventful day in the villages surrounding Stamford. In the days leading up to it, wild flowers and moss were gathered to decorate hoops, scooters, baskets and the mail cart for the May Queen. In Easton, decorating took place in the barn behind the Slater's Arms. Miss Baker took care of all the arrangements and Mr Morris would donate crown imperials to top off the hoops. When the big day arrived, the girls would parade round the village in white frocks and straw hats, singing *Now the Month is Maying* or *The Cuckoo is a Pretty Bird*, and occasionally dancing around the maypole. The money raised would be used to treat the children on Empire Day in March.

Opposite below: Maypole dancing at Kingscliffe Endowed School *c.* 1950. The Maypole is erected in the garden of the headmaster's house, which was an integral part of the school buildings until the mid-1970s.

Collyweston School children gather around the May Day decorated hoop, *c.* 1934. From left to right. back row: J. Jackson, J. Goodes, D. McLennon, T. Ridlington, T. Jackson, G. Barnes, C. Sharman, J. Bollins, B. Archer, A. Harrison. Second row right: J. Woods, H. Woods, M. Hament, B. Skellet, E. Jackson, R. Jackson (later publican of the Blue Bell who died in the Second World War, P. Watton. Second row left: G. Casterton, V. James, M. Hand, C. Ridlington, S. Roberts, I. Close, A. Woods, T. Wooley, R. Grundy, G. Spires, T. Popple, M. Osbourne, D. Smith, A. Casterton, J. Spires, M. Townsend. Front row: M. Knapp, W. Hand (behind), D. Knapp, G. Townsend, A. Grundy, H. Knapp, D. Casterton, E. Woods, H. Jones, D. Smith, E. Neal, J. Welby.

Opposite below: Geeston children returning home from Ketton School, *c.* 1906. Rhyming games were particularly popular with children during this period before the First World War, one of which involved a group forming a semi-circle and a child pointing to each in turn while reciting the rhyme:

> Inky Pinky, pen and ink,
> I can smell a great big stink.
> And it comes from you.

This caused undoubted embarrassment to the selected victim. Those were more innocent times!

School children playing on the A43 road through Collyweston, *c.* 1906. Such a limited volume of traffic passed through the village at this time that some of the elderly residents could remember running out in excitement to see a motor car pass by. Sports days were held here until the 1920s, and a responsible person would be put in charge of monitoring the road for traffic.

Empire Day, St Martin's School, 24 May 1908. On this day children assembled round the flagpole in the playground and saluted the raising of the Union Jack while singing empire songs. They

were taught to be proud of the British Empire.

Above left: In the early fourteenth century the Gilbertine monastic order had a hall in Stamford where advanced teaching took place. It is also speculated that St Leonard's Priory may have served a similar function. In 1333, however, a number of students, discontented with the conditions at Oxford University, formed a short-lived establishment in Stamford. This is a photograph of the copy of the Brazenose knocker in St Paul's Street, which commemorates this event.

Above right: Brazenose Gate, named after Brazenose College, Oxford. It is popularly believed to be the place where Oxford students set up a rival university in the fourteenth century.

People from Collyweston celebrate the coronation of King George VI, *c.* 1937. On the side of the float is a placard with these words inscribed:

Grow more potatoes
Save more bread
Then the hungry nations
Will be better fed.

The driver is Norman Skellet; the others are: Monica Woods, Mrs Goodman, Roy Jackson, William (Bill) Archer.

A photograph of the Dolby Float at King George VI's coronation, Wednesday 12 May 1937. It was taken by Mr Dolby.

Crowds gather outside Browne's Hospital, Broad Street, awaiting the proclamation of George VI as King, 6 May 1910.

Wombwell's Menagerie Parade at the start of Stamford Mid-Lent Fair, in the 1890s. By 1840 George Wombwell's famous menagerie, which was based in Scotland, had the largest collection of animals in the United Kingdom. It included: leopards, bears, elephants, camels, and two lions called Wallace and Nero who were undoubtedly among those used for baiting with mastiffs and bulldogs. In 1841, a drunken farmer was mauled after being dragged by his arm into the enclosure. The distraught man was eventually released after a hot iron was applied to the animal's nose. After her husband's death in 1850, Ann Wombwell became the proprietor of the attraction which by now consisted of fourteen wagons (some of which were built by Hayes of Stamford), a huge stock of animals and a fine brass band. The entourage continued for another eighty-two years, until 1932 when the animals were rehoused in Whipsnade Zoo.

Opposite above: Wigden's Scenic at Stamford Lent Fair in Sheepmarket, *c.* 1910. This travelling fairground attraction continued to operate until recent years.

Opposite *below:* Stamford Mid-Lent Fair, *c.* 1910. Stamford's Mid-Lent Fair, which dates back to the eleventh century, is still held near Mothering Sunday. This was one of many fairs and markets which took place throughout the year. These included: Friday Cattle Market; Candlemass Fair; Mid-Lent Fair; Horse Fair; Town Fair; Spring Fair for beasts and sheep; May Fair on the Monday after Corpus Christi; St Jame's Fair for beasts, horses, sheep and lambs; and St Simon and St Jude's Fair.

Stamford High Street, *c.* 1887. Flags and bunting announce the celebrations for Queen Victoria's Golden Jubilee.

The Union Jack and bunting are displayed in All Saints' Street to mark the relief of Mafeking, 17 May 1900. Lord Baden Powell's victory during the Boer War caused an outpouring of patriotism, and journalists at the time coined the phrase 'to Maffik'.

Crowd outside Eayres' grocery and provision store, No. 8 High Street, awaiting the result of the 1906 general election. The Liberal Party won with 49.4 per cent of the vote. A note on the back of this photograph announced that it was 'Good to see such a police presence'.

George Hotel in the 1920s. The exact age of this ancient coaching house is unknown, although a building belonging to the Abbots of Croyland possibly stood on this site in AD 947 . To have been in this ownership would make it at least 900 years old. As well as the frequent royal patronage over the centuries, many pilgrims are said to have been entertained here on their way to the Holy Land. The present building incorporates two religious houses which once stood at either side of the original small inn.

Above: The Fox Inn, Barnack, *c.* 1910. Mr Tippins the butcher lived in the house on the right, next door to the Wright sisters who ran a school from their home.

The Slater's Arms, The Lane, Easton –on-the-Hill, in around the 1890s. The figure in the foreground is believed to be Mrs Boughton, wife of Harry Boughton, who owned the inn from 1893 to 1904.

Opposite below: Willie Smith, publican, at the door of the Engine Inn, Collyweston, *c.* 1933. William Smith took over the Engine Inn with his wife in 1931. They continued until 1947 when both of them died. Their daughter became the licensee until the 1950s.

Collyweston High Street, *c*. 1906. On the left is the Corner Inn, run at the time by Richard Hill who later moved up the hill to become the publican of the Slater's Arms. On the right across the street is Buckworth's farmhouse which has since been demolished and given over to a paddock for Park Farm.

Exeter Arms, Stamford Road, Easton-on-the-Hill, in the early twentieth century. This pub had numerous changes of ownership between 1890 and the outbreak of the First World War. At the time of this photograph it is believed that Henry Shaw was the publican.

Crown Inn, Duddington, in the 1890s. Thomas Sanders, publican, stands at the door of his (later demolished) inn, which faced onto the Green.

Crown Hotel, All Saints' Place, *c.* 1865, The Crown Hotel, which was built in 1675, held a prominent position in the centre of town on the main coaching route from London to York. From the eighteenth to the early twentieth centuries it hired out gigs and dog carts as well as offering hospitality to weary travellers.

Horns and Blue Boar Inn, 12 Broad Street, *c.* 1860. Built in 1717, the inn drew its main clientele from the frequent markets and fairs which took place in that part of town. It was demolished in 1875 after the Beast Market moved across the river taking with it most of the potential customers. The two neighbouring pubs,The New Salutation (later the Stag and Pheasant), and the original Dolphin Inn, also ceased to exist at around this time.

Budding swimmers, *c.* 1936. Reverend Herbert Kearsley-Fry taking local children from Barnack village down to the river for swimming lessons. Note the safety precaution to prevent the youngsters from falling off the back of the vehicle.

Barrowden millstream. *c.* 1906. Boats were available for hire on this artificially created millstream, or leat, of the Welland leading up to Barrowden watermill.

Punting on the river Welland from the meadows with the town bridge in the background, *c.* 1900. Punting as a leisure activity only dates back to the late nineteenth century. Prior to this it was a mode of transport used in shallow, marshy regions for hunting wildfowl.

Above: Collyweston football team in the year that they won the Stamford Amateurs Cup, *c.* 1946, taken at Wothorpe Road football ground prior to the match against Ryhall.. The line up includes: secretary A. Smith, T. Bradshaw, J. Parsons, G. Burbidge, skipper T. Woolley, L. Deegan, P. Smith, K. Kettle, G. Barnes, T. Curlew, P. Bradshaw and J. Dawkins.

Above: Members of Collyweston cricket team. c. 1947. From left: F. Hubbard, Mr Guffick (schoolmaster), G. Burbage, T. Wooley.

Right: Easton-on-the-Hill Choral Society's production of *Aladdin and Out*, c. 1929. From left to right, back row: Frank Hubbard, Ernest Hand, Mr Morgan. Front row: Ted Stevenson, -?-, -?-, Harold Davies.

Opposite below: Collyweston Social Club, in the 1940s. The ladies relax after a cricket match against Duddington in Tixover. From left to right: chairman A. Harrod, H. Knapp, B. Knapp, P. Jackson, D. Spires, G. Green, I. Nash, Mrs Kirk, E. Close, Mrs Dennis, J. Sauntson, Mrs Gregory.

Easton-on-the Hill Quoits Team, *c.* 1910. From left to right: H. Nichols, B. Hubbard, T. Chappel, G. Brittain, F. Henson, 'Buzz' Nichols, F. Morgan, S. Hubbard. The face at the window behind is I. Hubbard.

The original quoits still in the possession of Mrs J. Chapman, *née* Hubbard. These solid iron rings, weighing between two to five pounds each, would be pitched a distance of eighteen yards with the intention of looping them around pegs in the ground set within a 3ft-square box.

An idyllic pastoral scene from Stamford meadows in the early twentieth century. St Martin's church is clearly evident in the background as it towers above the surrounding buildings.

Relaxing outside Duddington schoolhouse, *c.* 1930s. From left: C. Ellis, S. Hornby, J. Cooke, S. Winkles.

The Close family from Collyweston on a trip to the White Horse Inn at Deeping Gate, *c.* 1920s. A rather more expensive and luxurious alternative to using public transport, at a time when very few people owned a private car, was to hire a vehicle complete with chauffeur from Wheatley's Garage in Scotgate.

Central Cinema, in the 1930s. In 1925, Blackstones sold their showrooms to the Cambridge Cinema Company who completely refurbished it as a luxurious cinema capable of accommodating 615 people. This, however, was destroyed by fire in 1927 and the new Central Cinema, in classic art deco style, was built in its place. The first manager of the new cinema was Mr K. Friese-Greene, son of the famous pioneer of cinematography.

seven

Body and Soul

Left: St Mary's church restoration, *c.* 1913. The entire church was reconstructed around the thirteenth century tower, and is shown here under restoration. The 163ft spire was added in the fifteenth century.

Below: This is the ancient weathercock from the top of St Mary's spire after it was removed for renovation, *c.* 1913. It measures 80cm long and is made of cast brass. The tail of sheet copper was a later addition.

Opposite above: St Michael's church, Stamford High Street, *c.* 1910. There has been a church on this site since the twelfth century. A medieval building, which replaced this, survived until 1832 when it collapsed during renovation. The new church, which still stands, was deconsecrated in 1970 and given over to commerce. A number of shops still occupy the building.

Below: All Saints' church, *c.* 1897, which lies to the west of the original Danish Burgh and dates back to the eleventh century. Very little of the original building remained following devastation by Lancastrian forces in 1461. The Browne family, who are immortalised in brasses within the church, carried out extensive and lavish restoration including the magnificent tower and spire in perpendicular style. William Stukley, the great antiquarian, was vicar here from 1730 to 1747.

Above: St Martin's church, *c.* 1873. This building dates from the late fifteenth century, replacing an earlier medieval church, neither of which survive in the present structure. Very little, however, has been altered since this time. Inside the church there is a magnificent renaissance monument to the first Lord Burghley, chief advisor to Elizabeth I, who died in 1598. In the churchyard behind the church lie the remains of one of the area's most well-known characters, Daniel Lambert, who died here in 1809.

St Luke's church tower, Tixover, *c.* 1930. This church stands, unusually, approximately half-a-mile outside of the village along a farm track. This is popularly believed to be evidence of a previous settlement, abandoned perhaps due to plague. The truth, however, is probably less romantic in that the original main road through the village passed close to the church. This was moved in the late eighteenth century and eventually became the A47 which skirts the southern edge of the village. Inside the church are some interesting stone seats which were provided for the aged and infirm, at a time before wooden pews were provided for the comfort of all the congregation.

Opposite below: St Mary the Virgin's church, Morcott. This photograph, from the turn of the twentieth century, clearly shows the raised churchyard above the heads of the children. This is believed to be an indication of great age and possibly pre-dates the present church building, which is of twelfth century origin, although extensive restoration took place in 1874.

Left: Barrowden Baptist Chapel. This is a photograph of the building after its closure in 2003. There is a blue plaque on the outside dedicated to Thomas Cook, who preached here as an itinerant missionary in the early nineteenth century. In 1829 he married Marianne Mason, a farmer's daughter from Barrowden. Unable to make a living from his ministry, he became a woodturner and cabinet maker before moving to Market Harborough in 1833. In 1841 he and his family hired a train to take some Temperance supporters to a rally in Loughborough. This was the foundation of the Thomas Cook Travel Agency.

Below: St Peter's church, Barrowden, *c.* 1906. Barrowden church in Rutland practices the custom of 'Rushbearing', which dates from medieval times when the church was donated the gift of a nearby field. This bequest came with the condition that every year on St Peter's Day the church floor should be covered with rushes from the given pasture. Due to a scarcity of suitable rushes, the tradition died out soon after the First World War, but it was revived again recently.

St Leonard's Priory, *c.* 1873. This was originally a Benedictine monastery founded between 1080 and 1140, and is among the earliest of Stamford's many monastic buildings, others of which included Franciscans, Dominicans and Carmelites until the dissolution. Its initial use was as an administrative centre for Durham Cathedral, which held estates in the area.

St Peter's or All Saints' Callis, No. 13 All Saints' Street, in the 1890s. This was an almshouse for three poor women who resided there and received 6s each per week. The word 'callis' derives from Calais, where many of the wool merchants were based. It was rebuilt in 1863 with lodgings on two storeys, the upper being reached by an external stone staircase and covered timber gallery on the rear or south elevation.

Above left: Originally a hospital for the relief of travellers and the local poor, Burghley Almshouses to St Martin's Bede House were bought in 1549 by the lord treasurer to Queen Elizabeth I, Lord Burghley, who endowed it with £100 yearly which was to be used in the maintenance of a warden and twelve poor men. Pictured here around 1950 it stands at the southern end of the town bridge on a twelfth century culvert over the river Welland. Thomas Biller and John Wingfield also donated money in perpetuity for nurses and the upkeep of the buildings.

Above right: Medieval alms box from Browne's Hospital.

Left: Brass rubbing of William Browne. The Browne family, who carried out good work throughout the town, are immortalised in brass reliefs in All Saints' church. William, founder of the great hospital/almshouse, carried out extensive restoration to the church in the fifteenth century.

Opposite above: Browne's Hospital prior to reconstruction in 1869. This magnificent almshouse was founded in 1485 by the wealthy Stamford wool merchant William Browne. On the pavement in front stood six arcades under which the corn market was held. But the open corn exchange was not the most comfortable of buildings in which to trade the result of a year's labours, so the present corn exchange was erected. Three complete arches were moved: one to the entrance of the Congregational Hall in Star Lane, one to the entrance of the Bluecoat School, and one to the entrance to the garden of No. 30 Saint Paul's Street.

Browne's Hospital was completely restored and reconstructed by James Fowler of Louth. The gatehouse was moved north to become a porch which lined up with the cloister. The octagonal bell tower and turret was added to the south-west corner.

Browne's uniform, early twentieth century. Browne's Hospital was intended to accommodate twelve poor men and two women, one warden and a confrater. Men and women would receive 7s per week each for clothing, medical treatment and attendance.

Opposite above: Stamford Infirmary was erected in 1828 at a cost of £8000, which was raised by subscription with an endowment of £7477 by Mr Henry Fryer. Thomas Billen gave a rent charge of £16 in perpetuity to employ two women to act as nurses.

Opposite below: Infirmary Gate, the west gate of the Carmelite or White Friar's College. It was founded in the reign of Henry III.

St John's Ambulance Brigade members, *c.* 1926, after moving from a temporary headquarters in the Albert Hall, High Street, Stamford, to their current building in North Street. They formed in 1924, when ambulance brigade was a misnomer for the rather poorly funded group who used a four-wheeled cart, known as a 'hardtruck', to transport patients to the local hospital.

Fire brigade in front of the Stamford headquarters, in the 1920s. They are proudly displaying the trophies which they won in the escape and manual drills in the north-eastern district competitions. From left to right: T. Middleton, B.T. Grimes, W. Goodley, A. Bacon, H. Goodley, J. Hagger, G. Grimes.

Fire engine, *c.* 1904. A steamer in Bath Row. On 28 March the Stamford Fire Brigade invited local dignitaries to a demonstration of their newly acquired Shand Mason Steamer. The vehicle, which was still drawn by a team of horses, was much lighter than previous models. The steam engine was used to power a pump which was capable of producing a jet of water up to 160 feet high.

Above left: This picture, *c.* 1904, shows chief fire officer Robert W. Gibson, who was a founder member of the Stamford fire brigade in around 1841. At the time it was a private service costing £3 for an engine call out, £1 an hour for the brigade, and an extra charge for any horses. The cost would be met by either the victim or an insurance company. Gibson remained with the service until 1910.

Above right: Police constable Norris, in the 1860s. He was born on 6 October 1838 in North Lincolnshire and was a member of the Lincolnshire/Stamford Constabulary from 1866-71.

Fire at Greatford Hall. On 8 September 1822 at 4.30 a.m. a disastrous fire gutted the sixteenth-century Greatford Hall. The alarm, which was raised by a kitchen maid, brought people rushing from the nearby village eager to help save some of the contents of the house. Before the fire brigade arrived a number of valuable paintings and other goods were rescued from the blaze. By this time, however, the flames had reached the gun room causing the ammunition to explode. Some of the domestic staff were forced to escape by tying sheets together in order to climb from upper storey windows. Two sisters, Eva and Gladys Palmer from Belmsthorpe, were not so fortunate and, being trapped by the conflagration, had to hurl themselves onto the gravel below. Both survived the fall and were immediately transported to the local hospital.

Opposite above: Fire rages through Burley-on-the-Hill House near Oakham, *c.* 1904. The new steamer was used to extinguish the great fire at Burley-on the Hill House while the owner was entertaining Sir Winston Churchill. It is said that the great man hampered the efforts of the fire team by insisting on personally directing operations. Eventually, after a heated discussion, he was made to leave the brigade to carry out their duties unhindered. From that day on the engine was nicknamed Winston.

Opposite below: Royal Observer Corps, *c.* 1941. From left ro right, back row: W. Stafford, C. Skellet, S. Chambers, T. Chambers, W. Mitchell, D. Knapp, D. Wooley, H. Close. Front row: L. Bliss, W. Ealy, H. Thomas, A. Harrod, F. Maple, L. Mould, A. Cropley.

Re-interring Friar John, Broad Street, 7 October 1909. On Thursday 9 September 1909 workmen carrying out drainage operations at 7 Adelaide Street discovered a lead coffin. Through the hole pierced by a workman's pickaxe, it was possible to see human remains wrapped in a waxed canvas sheet. Placed carefully on the body was a parchment which was later identified as an indulgence from Pope Boniface IX to John Staunford. On first inspection the body was identified as that of Joan, Maid of Kent, the wife of Edward Black Prince. But a closer investigation at the British Museum revealed a red beard and a tonsure obviously belonging to a man of the cloth. This, together with the evidence from the folded parchment, clearly identified the remains as those of Friar John Staunton. A re-interment was carried out during which crowds paraded along Broad Street to the Catholic area of Stamford Cemetery, where the medieval monk was laid to rest.

eight

Local People, Local Events

Miss May Day, daughter of Neville Day and Frances Charlton, *c.* 1912. This was three years before her marriage to Reverend P.L. Hooson of Easton-on-the Hill. She died in 1920.

Above left: Annie Blackman fetching water from a public standpipe set into the wall of No. 31 West Street, Kingscliffe, *c.* 1948. Mrs Blackman lived in a cottage opposite and this photograph was taken by her young nephew Gilbert Markley with his box Brownie camera, a rarity in the village at that time. The standpipe replaced a public water pump provided in 1902 by the then owner of Windmill House (now No. 31 West Street). In 1914, piped water was brought to Kingscliffe from a reservoir at Apethorpe Hall which connected to a network of public standpipes at regular intervals along the village streets. But it was not until the early 1950s that a mains water supply was connected to every property in the village.

Above right: Atton Martin, farmer from Racecourse Road, Easton-on-the-Hill, in the early twentieth century.

Richard Branston, the gamekeeper for Burghley Estates, displays the trophies of his profession in Hillside Wood, *c.* 1928. He lived at the Gamekeeper's Lodge, Tinwell Drift, Easton-on-the-Hill.

Cabinet photograph of Arthur and Elizabeth Close, shortly after they were married, *c.* 1891. The painted pastoral landscape in the background was one of many alternative settings offered by photographers at this time.

Clara Merry outside Walnut Farmhouse in Stretton, at the turn of the twentieth century. Standing outside with Mrs Merry's sheep are the Sheffield children. Clara's daughter Mary remembers her mother making 'frumenty'. This was a kind of porridge made of hulled wheat which was boiled in milk and flavoured with sugar and spices.

Sam Mease from Duddington, *c.* 1865, who was a carrier from the Boat Inn on Tuesday, Thursday and Saturday. Note his missing leg which was possibly lost in the Crimean War, ten years before this photograph was taken.

'Glenville', Church Street, Easton-on-the-Hill. Mrs Mary Anne Hill with Bruce, and her uncle, Mr William Perkins, with Ross, *c.* 1909.

'The Slaters', Church Street, Easton-on-the-Hill. Miss Mary Anne Hill and Mrs R.J. Hill with baby Florence, *c.* 1909.

Above left: Mary Hill, outside The Cottage in Church Street, Easton-on-the-Hill. This photograph is believed to have been taken from the upper storey of the house across the street rented by Mr Seckington, a talented local photographer who set up his business in the village in 1921. He also became the local postman in 1929.

Above right: Beekeeper Francis Perm of No. 13 Vine Street, Stamford, *c.* 1920.

Left: May Reading shining shoes outside the house that has since been demolished, in Mill Street, Duddington, in the 1930s.

Daniel Lambert, who died at the age of forty at 9.00 a.m. on the 21 June 1809, held the record for being England's fattest man. He died at the Wagon and Horses Inn, while visiting the racecourse in Easton-on-the-Hill. His considerable headstone bears the inscription:

In Remembrance of
That Prodigy in Nature.
Daniel Lambert,
a native of Leicester
who was possessed of
an exalted and convivial Mind
had no competition.
He measured three feet one inch around the leg, nine feet four inches round the body
and weighed
Fifty Two Stone Eleven Pounds.
He departed this life
on the 21st June 1809,
aged forty years.
As a Testimony of Respect
This Stone is erected
By his Friends
In Leicester.

Other local titles published by Tempus

Around Grantham

FRED LEADBETTER

With pictures from some of the most notable local photographers of the period, this captivating collection of more than 200 photographs and postcards will appeal to anyone with an interest in Grantham's history from the middle of the Victorian era until the 1960s. This selection of images savours Grantham's past while introducing newcomers and the younger generation to the area's history.

0 7524 1863 7

Leicester Voices

CYNTHIA BROWN

Alluring and absorbing, these personal memories of times past, selected from the East Midland Oral History Archive, provide a unique and valuable record of what life used to be like in Leicester. By recalling everyday life and events in the words of the people who experienced them first-hand, and illustrated by a wide selection of archive photographs, Leicester Voices provides a fascinating glimpse into the city's past

0 7524 2657 5

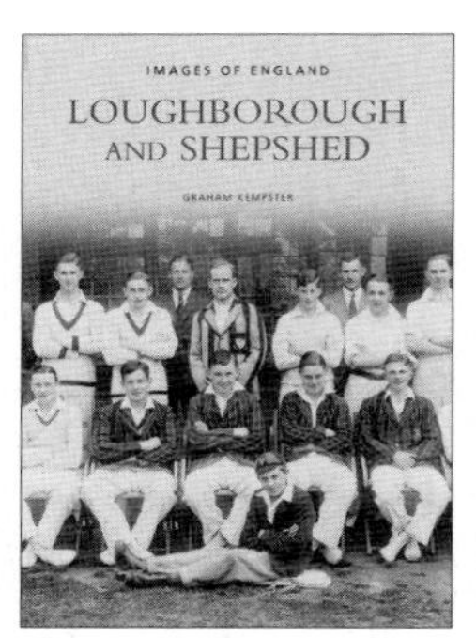

Loughborough and Shepshed

GRAHAM KEMPSTER

This intriguing selection of old images, drawn from over 100 years of the Loughborough Echo archives, traces some of the important changes and developments that have taken place in Loughborough and Shepshed during this period. Charting significant events, from the Coronation celebrations of 1902 to Shepshed Parade and Gala in 1950, there are also snapshots of everyday life, from schools and shops to sport and leisure pursuits, and, most importantly, the townspeople themselves.

0 7524 3252 4

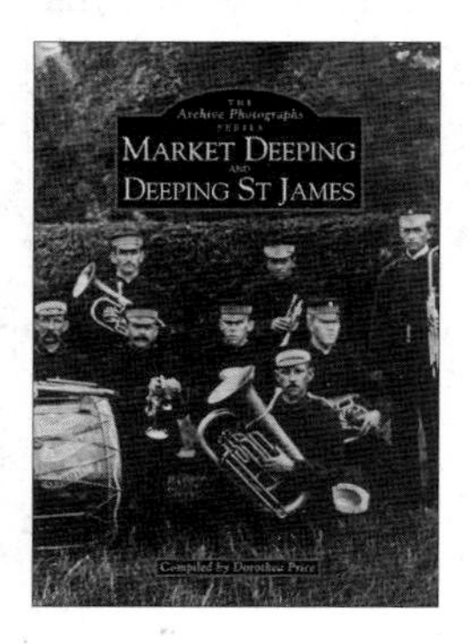

Market Deeping and Deeping St James

DOROTHEA PRICE

This fascinating collection of images vividly recollects the life, landmarks and people of the villages of Market Deeping and Deeping St James. Perhaps you can remember the Deeping Feast or have taken part in the Duck Derby or the Raft Race; you may have shopped at Dudney & Johnson's, Walter Smith's Unique Shopping Centre or Lambert & Kisby's. Whatever your memories, this evocative book will appeal to all those who know and love this corner of Lincolnshire.

0 7524 1096 2

If you are interested in purchasing other books published by Tempus, or in case you have difficulty finding any Tempus books in your local bookshop, you can also place orders directly through our website

www.tempus-publishing.com